How do I use this

Sometimes we need to create a space for ourselves to learn and unlearn certain principles, opinions and mindsets that we have been exposed to through experiences and circumstances.

It is important to remember that you hold the key to your own peace, calmness, and happiness in this life. In the process of decluttering thoughts and emotions for you to critically analyze and make mindset shifts, a therapeutic tool like journaling helps.

Journaling helps put your thoughts down on paper, eliminating doubts as your quest for self discovery has created a space for questions to be asked and answered. Journaling allows you to discover several layers and versions of yourself. Journaling prompts enable you to delve deep within yourself and examine how you think and feel.

Healing, transformation, empowerment and growth is possible when you open yourself for self discovery and self care. It is a gradual process with small steps taken everyday, each discovery linking to another to reset your thought patterns and redefine your approach to life.

You have taken the first step. No matter how challenging and painful this process might be, don't relent on your journey towards self improvement. Keep going!

I WILL LET GO OF
MY EXPECTATIONS
of perfection
AND ALLOW THINGS TO
happen imperfectly.

THIS IS THE SELF CARE JOURNEY OF:

_____

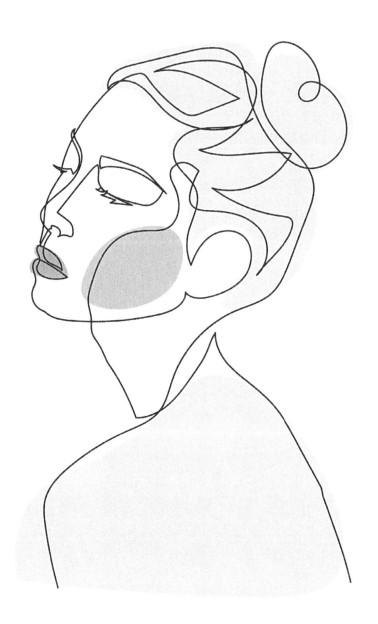

By trying to be perfect, I may hold myself to excessively high personal standards and overly critical self-evaluations. How can I respond to my inner perfectionist's expectations, demands and criticisms with understanding and compassion?

_____

_____

_____

_____

_____

_____

_____

_____

_____

_____

_____

_____

_____

_____

EVEN WHEN IT FEELS
CHAOTIC, THERE IS

peace and love

WITHIN ME.

Worry is a cascading series of negative thoughts. We start with "what if this happens" and then add, "and then what if that happens" and so on in a domino effect. How can I remind myself that my negative thoughts are not facts?

_____

_____

_____

_____

_____

_____

_____

_____

_____

_____

_____

_____

_____

_____

_____

_____

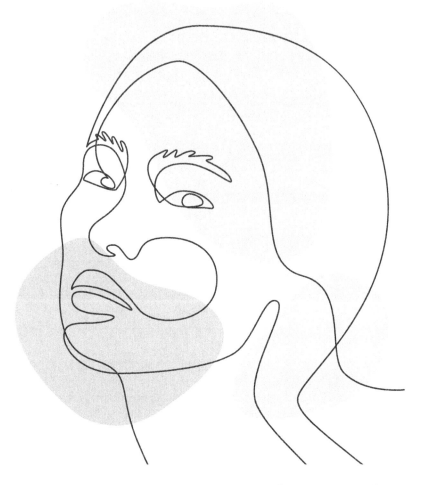

I HAVE THE STRENGTH TO

remain calm

EVEN IN THE MIDDLE OF

a storm.

When I am feeling anxious or stressed, naming what I am feeling may help my stress response to calm down. What made me anxious today? What are the names I would give these feelings?

_____

_____

_____

_____

_____

_____

_____

_____

_____

_____

_____

_____

_____

_____

I have faith
IN MY ABILITIES.
I know more
THAN I THINK I DO.

Recalling challenging times makes me see how far I have come. Let me recall a difficult experience that I went through and remember how I was able to overcome it.

_____

_____

_____

_____

_____

_____

_____

_____

_____

_____

_____

_____

_____

_____

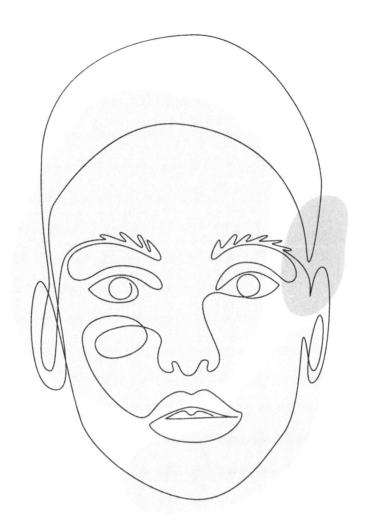

MY HEART IS OPEN.

I am willing

TO FORGIVE AND

start again.

Forgiveness is all about helping me so that I can be at peace. What does forgiveness mean to me? Am I forgiving towards myself and others? How can I learn to forgive and forget?

_____

_____

_____

_____

_____

_____

_____

_____

_____

_____

_____

_____

_____

_____

_____

_____

I let go of

NEGATIVE THOUGHTS AND
BEHAVIORS AS THEY

no longer serve me.

We tend to focus on our negative experiences and exaggerate their impact on our lives. What negative thoughts are limiting me today? What happens if I let these negative thoughts go?

_____

_____

_____

_____

_____

_____

_____

_____

_____

_____

_____

_____

_____

_____

_____

_____

I AM CAPABLE OF
amazing things
IF I BELIEVE AND ACT WITH
intention and purpose.

A sense of purpose is the motivation that drives me towards a satisfying future. What is my experience of life's meaning and purpose recently? How do I stay close to the truth and remember my why?

SOMETIMES I NEED

to say no

TO SAY YES

to myself.

What am I afraid of happening when I say 'no' to a person or activity? Am I seeking approval from others by saying 'yes' to everything? Or am I trying to avoid protests to my 'no'? How can I make my 'no' powerful and final?

I THINK THINGS THROUGH

first with grace

BEFORE REACTING.

Most decisions in my life don't have to be immediate. How do I relish in the joy of pondering? What can I do to train my mind to pause, listen and assimilate before reacting?

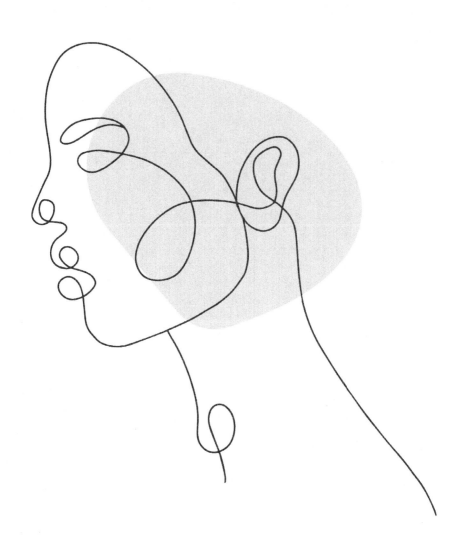

POSITIVITY IS A CHOICE

and I choose

TO BE POSITIVE.

Being positive doesn't mean I should ignore the negative moods and experiences in my life – just that I should try to balance them with positive ones. How can I shift my inner narrative to reflect this balance? What do I need to add or subtract?

I WILL TALK

to myself

THE WAY I TALK TO

someone I love.

Self love means accepting my emotions for what they are and prioritizing my physical, emotional and mental well-being. How can I cultivate a deeper connection with myself, which in turn can connect me with others?

I love myself as I am

AND WILL NOT EXPECT
PERFECTION IN ORDER

to love myself.

By giving unconditional support, self-care, and compassion to myself, I translate it to good health, great self-esteem, happiness, balance and well-being. How can I accept that I am equipped with uniqueness and abundance?

I AM THE ONLY PERSON

who can control

MY THOUGHTS AND ACTIONS.

Change is unsettling and generates fear and resentment. How do I navigate through change, uncertainty and the unknown? How can I be flexible and embrace the changes in my life?

_____

_____

_____

_____

_____

_____

_____

_____

_____

_____

_____

_____

_____

_____

_____

_____

I will not be afraid

OR EMBARRASSED

to ask for help.

Asking for help isn't easy, but it is necessary if I want to be as effective and productive as I know I can be. How do I stop feeling uneasy asking for help? How can I stop viewing it as a surrender of control or that I come across as incompetent?

_____

_____

_____

_____

_____

_____

_____

_____

_____

_____

_____

_____

_____

_____

_____

_____

EVERYTHING THAT IS

happening now

IS HAPPENING FOR

my ultimate good.

It is comforting to think that there is a purpose to going through difficult situations, and there will be a use for what I am going through. How can I be open to the pain and difficulty, to be truly open to gain from such experiences?

I CANNOT CHANGE OTHERS,

so I will love them

FOR WHO THEY ARE.

Acceptance is the ability to see that others have a right to be their own unique persons. That means having a right to their own feelings, thoughts and opinions. How can I accept others as they are, give them the space to find their own path and to learn their own truth?

I IMAGINE THE SOLUTIONS

rather than focusing

ON THE PROBLEMS.

A solution mindset focuses on solving problems, rather than getting stuck when challenges arise. How do I view problems as opportunities to grow rather than painful experiences? How do I inculcate the mindset of looking ahead and moving forward?

I am willing to learn

BECAUSE THE MORE I LEARN,

the more I grow.

When I view challenges as opportunities for learning, I develop a growth mindset. By changing the way I think, I can change the way I learn. How do I allow my life experiences to shape me and broaden my view of the world?

I LET GO OF THE STRUGGLE

and surrender to life

WITH A SENSE OF

inner peace.

I gain significant inner peace when I surrender to the process of change. How do I start the process of letting go of fear, worries and expectations and replacing them with mental space and the opportunity for clarity?

A river of compassion
WASHES AWAY MY ANGER TO
replace it with love.

Compassion is the quality that allows me to step outside of myself and see the circumstances of others. How can I release judgements of others and trust that life is hard and everyone is doing the best they can?

I WAS NOT BORN TO
stay the same.
EVOLUTION IS A PART
of my process.

When I am on a path towards self-evolution, I will be better prepared to handle challenges in life and all of the turmoil they can present. What are the small actions that I can take throughout my day to create a more evolved me?

TODAY, I ABANDON MY
old habits
AND TAKE UP NEW,
more positive ones.

Habits are learned. Therefore, I can unlearn bad habits and learn new, positive habits to replace those undesirable ones. What are the old habits that I wish to shed? What are the new ones that I will consciously take up?

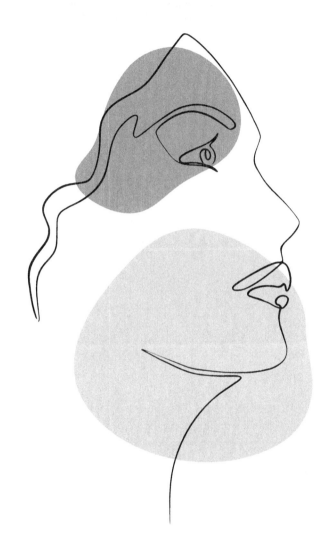

I nurture myself

FIRST SO I CAN GIVE

more to others.

When helping others, I need to give from a place of abundance – and I can't give what I don't have. How do I practice radical self care and nurture myself everyday? How do I understand that there is nothing indulgent or selfish about self care?

I HAVE
UNLIMITED POTENTIAL.

I am made for more.

When I believe in myself, my potential isn't something I need to reach; it's something waiting to be discovered. How do I become all that I have the possibility of becoming?

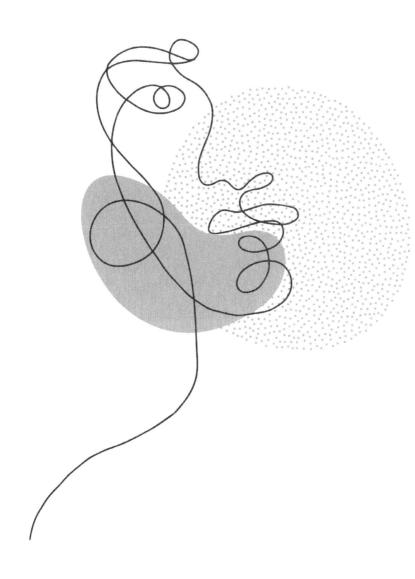

I AM IN CHARGE OF

how I feel today.

When I choose to give in to negativity and pessimism, I am missing out on an important opportunity for growth and development. How do I develop an attitude that focuses on the bright side of life and expect positive results?

_____

_____

_____

_____

_____

_____

_____

_____

_____

_____

_____

_____

_____

_____

I AM SO MUCH MORE THAN
my mistakes.
I AM GROWING
from my past.

I need to learn from my mistakes so that I do not run the risk of repeating them. How can I own my mistakes and let them be stepping stones to success in my life?

I am worthy
OF THE LOVE THAT
I pour into others.

When I start to love myself, I will stop seeking happiness outside of me. How do I cast out the idea that I have to be perfect to be loved? How do I start talking to and about myself in a loving way?

_____

_____

_____

_____

_____

_____

_____

_____

_____

_____

_____

_____

_____

_____

_____

_____

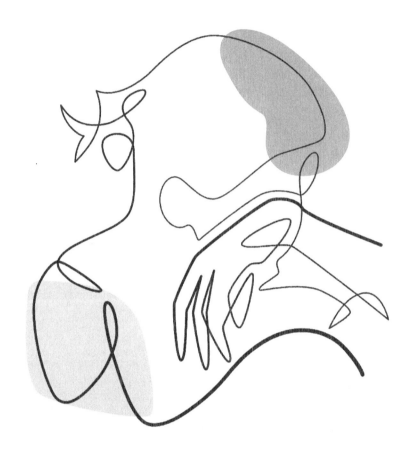

Love, forgiveness

AND UNDERSTANDING IS THE

very foundation

OF MY RELATIONSHIP.

Being able to forgive and to let go of past hurts is a critical tool in a relationship. How can I make a deliberate decision to put my partner's transgressions behind me, so that we can move forward together?

Today I will love

FIERCELY, LAUGH FREELY

and live courageously.

Living courageously involves shifting my focus from warding off fear to pursuing a full and meaningful life alongside of fear. How can I embrace my vulnerability, admit my fears to myself and live a life of confidence and freedom?

MY FEARS OF TOMORROW

are simply

MELTING AWAY.

If I can imagine the possibilities of a life without fear and realise that most of my fears are unreal, I can do just about anything. How can I embrace rational fears and manage my irrational fears so that I can live the real life I deserve?

_____

_____

_____

_____

_____

_____

_____

_____

_____

_____

_____

_____

_____

_____

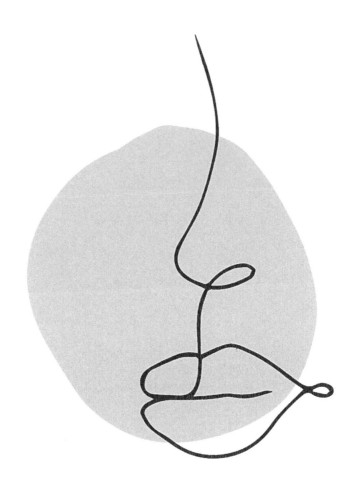

I will have fun

DOING THE MUNDANE TODAY.

To be authentically healthy, I need to find the balance between juggling adult responsibilities and enjoying simple happy pleasures. How do I seek joy in the ordinary and find pleasure in the mundane routine of my life?

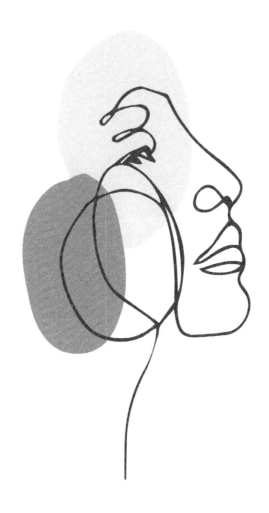

I AM THE ARCHITECT
of my life;
I BUILD IT'S FOUNDATION AND
choose it's contents.

I am capable of creating the circumstances of my own life by having control over every choice that I make. How do I take the first steps to design the life that I want?

_____

_____

_____

_____

_____

_____

_____

_____

_____

_____

_____

_____

_____

_____

Creative energy

SURGES THROUGH ME AND

leads me to

NEW AND BRILLIANT IDEAS.

Creative energy is a tireless impulse to absorb and discover new things, a drive to create and break boundaries, bring joy and connect to others. How do I activate the seeds of ideas, concepts, designs, stories and images that lie within me?

_____

_____

_____

_____

_____

_____

_____

_____

_____

_____

_____

_____

_____

_____

I ACCEPT MY EMOTIONS AND

let them serve

THEIR PURPOSE

Being aware of my emotions can help me talk about feelings more clearly, avoid or resolve conflicts better, and move past difficult feelings more easily. How do I allow my emotions to be what they are without judging them or trying to change them?

_____

_____

_____

_____

_____

_____

_____

_____

_____

_____

_____

_____

_____

_____

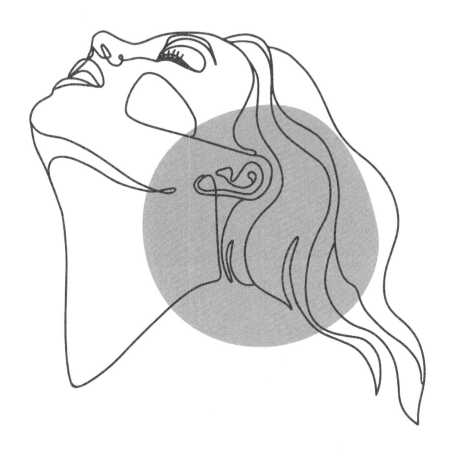

I WAKE UP TODAY WITH

strength in my heart

AND CLARITY IN MY MIND.

Mental clarity means having a focused and clear state of mind. When I have mental clarity, my mind isn't clouded with indecision, what-ifs or worry. What are the things that I can do to declutter my mind for clarity, focus, peace, and balance?

_____

_____

_____

_____

_____

_____

_____

_____

_____

_____

_____

_____

_____

_____

I accept where I am
IN LIFE AND WILL MAKE
the most of today.

My life is a collection of single days one right after the other. The sun rises, sets, and rises again. And in the end, the life I choose to live will be determined by how I choose to spend each day. How do I embrace each day individually and discover the potential that it holds?

My life is a gift

AND I APPRECIATE

everything I have.

The simple practice of expressing appreciation each day can move me into a new emotional state of self reflection and peace within myself. How do I explore all areas of giving, satisfaction and love through appreciation?

_____

_____

_____

_____

_____

_____

_____

_____

_____

_____

_____

_____

_____

_____

_____

I ALLOW MYSELF

to be who I am

WITHOUT JUDGMENT.

A lack of self-love can hold me back. It can prevent me from connecting with my purpose and doing great things. How can I cut myself some slack when I fall short of expectations?

My body is perfect

IN THE WAY IT IS

intended to be.

Loving my body, having an intimate relationship with my body, means taking good care of it. How do I catch myself when I am comparing my body to the bodies of others? How can I remind myself that my body is unique and beautiful in its own way?

_____

_____

_____

_____

_____

_____

_____

_____

_____

_____

_____

_____

_____

_____

I take care of

MY BODY, MIND, AND SOUL.

My body and mind are not two separate entities, and the health of one affects the health of the other. How do I reclaim the true meaning of self-care and self-love, and watch my life bloom?

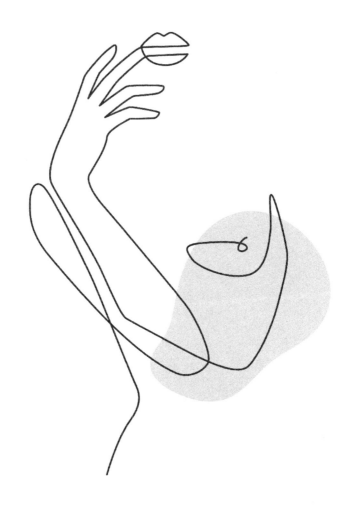

I CAN PREPARE FOR THE JOY

and heal from hurt

AT THE SAME TIME.

How do I cultivate my own inner peace and wisdom that allows me to see that my pain is part of the pain of all human beings universally, to reset my moral compass, and to remain compassionate even in the face of injustice, betrayal, and harm?

The challenges

I AM CONFRONTED WITH ARE

opportunities for growth.

How do I learn and grow from my challenges instead of becoming trapped or swallowed by them? How do I shape that transformation to help me move forward, instead of leaving me stuck?

I WILL ACHIEVE GREAT THINGS
through small steps.

I need to be content with the small steps that I take everyday so that when I look back down the road, it all adds up. How do I focus not on success but significance and that with time, even the small steps and little victories along my path will take on greater meaning?

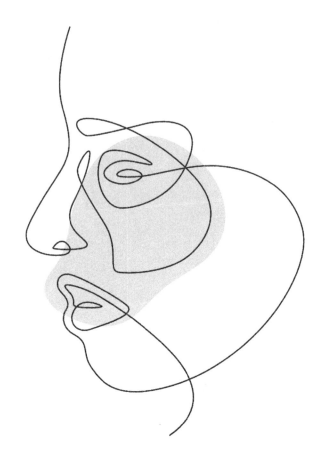

MY THOUGHTS ARE FILLED

with positivity

AND MY LIFE IS PLENTIFUL

with prosperity.

Harnessing the power of thought in a positive way has the ability to create great change in my life, including my financial well-being and prosperity. How do I develop a prosperity mindset where I see opportunities for growth and wealth creation in every challenging situation?

I'm allowed

TO TAKE THE TIME TO HEAL.

True healing occurs when I give myself permission to feel whatever feelings live below the triggers. How do I give my heart enough time to accept what my mind already knows? How do I be gentle and patient with myself?

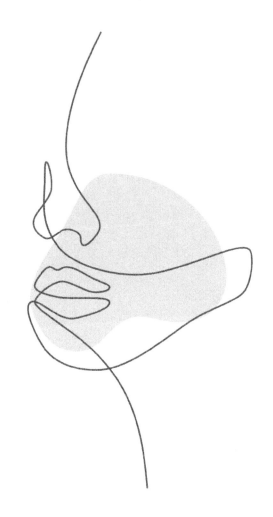

MY OBSTACLES ARE

moving out of my way;

MY PATH IS CARVED

towards greatness.

Once I begin to change the way I think, I will begin to inspire innovation that will help me to manifest greatness in my life. How can I make my vision so clear that my fears become irrelevant?

_____

_____

_____

_____

_____

_____

_____

_____

_____

_____

_____

_____

_____

I AM BECOMING CLOSER

to my true self

EVERY DAY.

My passion, drive and creativity lies within my authentic self, the one I have buried beneath other people's needs. How can I strip away the layers that I am identified with and expose the truth of who I really am?

I MAKE A DIFFERENCE

in the world

BY SIMPLY EXISTING IN IT.

My presence on this earth makes a difference whether I see it or not. Every second that I spend doubting my worth is a moment of my life thrown away. How do I wake up everyday feeling exceptional, important, needed and unique?

Printed in Great Britain
by Amazon